The Suffering of a Child

a family's journey through childhood terminal cancer

Heather So

The cover design reflects and incorporates Emily's favourite colours.

print ISBN 978-1-5271-1298-8
ebook ISBN 978-1-5271-1386-2

10 9 8 7 6 5 4 3 2 1

Published in 2025
by
Christian Focus Publications Ltd.,
Geanies House, Fearn, Ross-shire
IV20 1TW, Great Britain.

www.christianfocus.com

Cover design by James Amour

Printed and bound by
Bell and Bain Glasgow

This book is an open window to a mother's heart and soul as she is reluctantly taken on the painful journey of her precious daughter's decline, suffering and death. For anyone experiencing the loss of a child or caring for others traversing a similar path, Heather's journal may help provide the words you cannot find or know how to say.

David Clarke
Senior Minister, Hoxton Park Anglican Church,
Sydney, Australia

This book is eye opening, intense and heartbreaking. As health professionals we walk with many patients who suffer, deteriorate and die, yet nothing is so horrible as a sudden unbeatable cancer in a young child – such was the case with Emily So, whom I knew personally as her GP. No training in medical school teaches us how to care for a patient in such a circumstance; we are clueless unless we ourselves have experienced it.

I highly commend this book to anyone, including health professionals, who has journeyed with someone with terminal cancer. It will illuminate your perspective and give hope when there is no other medical hope.

Dr Kylie Chu
General Practitioner, New South Wales, Australia

Grief is a strange affliction. It robs you of many things, sometimes most tragically, the ability to express the sorrow of an aching heart. *The Suffering of a Child* invites us into a raw and intimate expression of unfathomable loss and leads us to lay our grieving hearts at the feet of Jesus. Whether you are suffering or trying to understand the sorrow of someone you love, this brief book is beyond useful.

Garrett Kell
Pastor, Del Ray Baptist Church, Alexandria, Virginia

For my three daughters.

Contents

Foreword

The death of a child is a tragedy. To bury one's own child is universally viewed as a distortion of the normal shape of life. The bereavement is magnified as it represents a loss not only of a treasured relationship, but also the hopes and dreams for a life cut short. In this book Heather So shares the diary she kept as her daughter Emily slowly died from terminal cancer, documenting the journey of grief for those in Emily's world, as well as the suffering of Emily herself.

The experience of significant loss is known to universally precipitate existential questions which can be difficult for us to answer – questions such as, where is God in our suffering? How can we possibly cope with this? This is so unfair, why has it happened to us? Such questions are challenging for anyone. How much more so when asked on behalf of one's child. Questions such as these require spiritual resources to find a meaning in life that allows us to persevere through the darkest of valleys, to give us hope that we can endure through that which appears to be unendurable.

The repeated referral to Scripture as the compass that helps Heather and her family navigate the storm is a witness to the faithfulness of the one who knows what it is to lose a beloved child. At a time when nothing makes sense, here is a witness that the Father of compassion and the God of all comfort can uphold us in our grief and carry our heaviest burden. It may not make our experience less painful, but it saves us from despair. Here is meaning, in the shape of a cross.

This is why it is so important that we remember the spiritual needs of those approaching the end of life. It is wonderful that friends and family rally with offers of meals and well wishes. Of course it is important for healthcare staff to provide accurate diagnoses, and offer the best possible treatments. But with any major health crisis, spiritual needs will also need to be addressed. Spiritual care is irreplaceable in this setting, and we are negligent if we do not ensure its provision.

This is not a comfortable book to read. Heather So is devastatingly honest about the experience for herself and those around her, and it is difficult to witness. This is naked lament in all its pain and fury. Staying with suffering can challenge us deeply, and we can understand why so many people resort to determined cheerfulness in the face of a hopeless prognosis. It helps us cope. It helps us ignore our anxiety about death. It doesn't help those suffering.

We are told to mourn with those who mourn. Heather's courage gives us the rare privilege of gaining insight into how those of us on the outside can best empathise and support those walking this challenging path. As such, I consider it essential reading not only for those who have lost someone close, but also pastoral workers and healthcare professionals in the end of life space. We cannot answer the existential questions on behalf of those who suffer, they must do the work themselves, but with the gracious help of those who have been there, we can learn a lot about how we can be a blessing, rather than a burden, as we walk alongside.

Megan Best
Associate Professor, Institute for Ethics and Society,
University of Notre Dame Australia
March 2024

Introduction

If there is a meaning in life at all,
then there must be a meaning in suffering.
Suffering is an ineradicable part of life,
even as fate and death.
Without suffering and death,
human life cannot be complete.
(Frankl, p. 76)

I started writing about suffering and death soon after Emily, my youngest daughter, was diagnosed with terminal cancer. Emily was only four years old when we learned she had a rare, aggressive, and incurable brain tumour.

On the second night after receiving her diagnosis, huddled into her hospital bed, I started talking to Emily about the gospel story. Emily listened quietly, and then responded, "Mummy, I think if I go to heaven and none of my family is there, I will be lonely". I was shocked into silence, realising for the first time that even though we hadn't said anything directly to Emily yet, she must already know that she was dying. Maybe she could feel it in her body. I couldn't speak from the lump in my throat and tears in my eyes, so I held her tightly until we fell asleep.

The next morning, I found Emily inconsolably crying on her hospital bed. In just a few short days, she'd gone from being a normal, happy four-year-old at preschool to being confined to a hospital bed – poked, prodded, scanned, examined, and woken up by nurses for observations throughout the night. Robbed of her normal childhood experience, and confronted by her own mortality, Emily had started sobbing deeply and was hugging me tightly on the hospital bed. Cradled in my lap, the cries came from deep inside of her; they were a cry from the soul.

A doctor, on hearing Emily's sobs, came into our room and asked me what her crying was about. I said to him, "I think this is existential pain more than physical pain". The doctor looked at me wide-eyed and said "Oh…" then quickly changed the subject. Following this, he hastily exited and left us alone. I was stunned. My weeping daughter was staring straight at her suffering; I hardly knew what to say to her and this health professional had run away.

This feeling of awkwardness and being unprepared is understandable: suffering and death are often ignored in Western society. Other ages of human history were closer to death and suffering, whereas with our modern approach to life and medicine, the very sick are often moved away from the home, and the death of a child is rare. That too was my experience. Until death came for my child.

Over the seven months of Emily's suffering, and the three months following her passing, I started waking at 5.00 a.m. almost every morning. At this early hour, I started to write down events I was observing. I also read from authors who had suffered greatly in life or who had looked deeply into the subject. Throughout Em's journey, I confided in many close family and friends, particularly my husband. As a family, we also met together for a time of daily 'devotion' which involved reading, reflection, and prayer each evening. This short journal is the outcome of that time.

The journal reflects on my outward and inner experiences during Emily's childhood terminal cancer and death. Like ripples in water, I observed that what Emily endured rolled over many people in different ways. So, this journal is arranged from my perspective first, then observations around my marriage, my other children, our community, and health professionals. Finally, the climax of this journal is my observations of Emily herself, and then a reflection on my initial thoughts on what we have been given through this season.

My reflections come from my roles within my family as a wife, mother, and full-time carer. I also write from my perspective as a Christian and an occupational therapist (OT) within the Australian context. While all the recollections aim to be truthful, I have tried to protect the privacy of those around me. The stories including my husband and two older children have been used with their permission. I collected these short journal entries over ten months much like a mosaic, pulling together the fragments into loose themes. Therefore, the journal entries switch back in time with each new chapter, as they were written and organised thematically, rather than chronologically.

At the centre of this journal is my Emily, so I wanted to introduce her briefly. Throughout her short life, Em remained a delightful enigma, always doing life in her own way. One of her nicknames in the family was 'Captain Random' because we never knew what she would choose to do next. She was constantly engaged in new craft creations, or pretend play. She loved the inflatable wobbly men at car dealerships, and lighthouses that one could walk up on the inside. Most of all, she loved elephants, and especially her favourite toy elephant 'Ellie'.

Emily was an introvert, and she called herself "shy". She had a small inner circle, with whom she was chatty and funny. She was also stubborn and strong in her sense of herself. In preschool she refused to borrow any *children's* library books from the school library and insisted on reading only encyclopaedias. Yet even though Em was naturally intelligent she was uninterested in people's praise of her. She enjoyed her accomplishments for her own sake.

Emily also had a gentle and affectionate spirit. In the latter months of her disease, she slowly lost many of her functions, including the ability to walk. One day at home I walked in with a tray full of takeaway drinks for us, and I fumbled it and dropped two of the drinks all over the living room floor in front of Em. Instead of laughing at me, Em gently reassured me, "Don't worry Mummy, I find walking really hard too".

That was our Emily, our free-spirited little girl. This is a compilation of the journal entries I wrote during the crisis of slowly losing her to cancer. This book represents my own imperfect response to an overwhelming situation. It is a story, a tribute, a critique, and a lament. Overall, it is a grappling in faith with one of the cruellest events to witness: the suffering and death of a child.

> Her absence is like the sky, spread over everything.
> (Lewis, p. 12)

1

BRACING

Reflections concentrating on my experience as Emily's mother, from the time of Emily's diagnosis until just prior to her death.

Sometimes it seemed to him that his life was delicate as a dandelion. One little puff from any direction, and it was blown to bits.
(Paterson, p. 108)

In the periphery

November 2021

Emily's sickness started developing in our periphery, during the second COVID-19 lockdown. A month before diagnosis, we took the three girls to a local park to try to teach Emily how to ride her bike without training wheels. Emily was four years old; her sisters were six and eight. While her two older sisters whipped around on their scooters, Emily couldn't balance the bike for even a second. In that moment, I busied myself thinking of balance activities to help her. That day, and over the following month, I saw symptoms in her, but I drew the wrong conclusions.

Two Sundays later, Emily was watching a video call and vomited all over the living room floor. Just one random vomit. Five days later, we drove twenty minutes in the car, and she threw up. Two days later, it happened again. After all this, I was thinking Emily may have car sickness and visual problems. I rang our behavioural optometrist the next morning and made her an appointment.

That Monday was also the first day back at school after four months of lockdown, and the girls had been nervous and excited about going back. Then the school rang me at lunchtime – Emily had fallen asleep at her desk. "Was this normal?" Now I was unsure what was going on with Emily, but I was determined to get on top of it. I decided to book in with our family doctor after I'd seen the behavioural optometrist. I talked to a few more OT friends for their advice, and I pulled together a therapy program from my resources. I was a bit rattled, but I would handle this for Emily.

Then Wednesday morning came, and Emily started vomiting until she dry wretched. She had no temperature. I rang my husband B.J. at his work (he is a doctor), and together we went to the children's hospital. At the hospital, we waited for eight hours in the Emergency Department. The junior doctor was friendly but was unsure what was wrong. Emily looked unsteady on her feet, but that could have been because she'd been vomiting all day. The junior doctor offered me admission or discharge for Emily – it was "my choice". I said admission, because "my husband would want that". Emily fell asleep in my arms in the hospital bed, and B.J. came in to take over.

On Thursday morning, the doctors' noticed Emily was unable to move her eyes to the side. Concerned by this, they organised an urgent MRI scan of Emily's brain that day. At this stage, I was still thinking that the most likely reason for her vomiting was a virus. Yet as I was driving into the hospital at about 6 p.m. that evening, I called B.J., and suddenly everything became much more serious. He sounded strange on the phone,

"The test results are back and it's bad. Just get here *now*".

My Baby

November 2021

I made it to the children's hospital and was brought to the theatre recovery area. A paediatrician met us in a small side room with his senior trainee. B.J. was sitting across from them, visibly upset. The atmosphere in the room was heavy, and immediately I felt on edge, wanting to catch up on whatever everybody else already knew.

The paediatrician broke the news – "Emily has diffuse intrinsic pontine glioma, or DIPG". I didn't recognise those words, so I had to double check we were talking about cancer. "Yes, it is cancer, and it is rare." Apparently, there was no way we could have picked it up any earlier because this type of cancer is aggressive and fast growing. The cancer had spread throughout her brain stem, so it was inoperable. The diagnosis is terminal. They could offer Emily radiotherapy to buy her some more time, but the average prognosis for most children was only six to nine months.

At this point, B.J. started breaking down crying, his head in his hands, and I could no longer hear what the doctor was saying. I felt out of my body for a lot of that conversation. People were talking at me like I still had all my mental capacities; I did not. The shock made me unable to hear properly, and underneath all the conversations, my soul kept breaking into an internal weeping mantra, "My baby, my baby, my baby…".

Anger

November 2021

After the first days of shock and disbelief wore off, an anger has woken up deep inside of me. My baby. *My* baby. Friends and family are calling me, crying on the phone. But I feel myself standing back from their tears. I am not falling apart; I am tense. I can feel a rage in me that I have not known before.

Everyday Em sobs for the whole forty-minute car trip into the hospital. She will undergo thirty daily sessions of radiotherapy over six weeks. She tells me every morning that she is scared, and that she doesn't understand why we have to do this. Every time it's my turn to take her into the hospital, she tries to hide into my arms as the nurses and doctors talk to her, and as they put her under another general anaesthetic. Every day she wakes up from her treatment with more fatigue and symptoms. She is getting worse, not better – the doctors don't understand it. And after this round of initial treatment is done, how many more months will we get with her? Will we have to turn to experimental clinical trials? How hard will we have to fight a losing battle?

I am angry, and this new anger is not like other angers; it is maternal, primitive, protective. I feel I am wrestling with God for Emily's life, and I know I will probably lose. God could have stopped the cancer from growing, but He didn't.

I feel angry that we have to force Emily through daily scary treatment that she doesn't understand. Angry that I feel in some way complicit in her many daily sufferings: having to hold her down, cajoling her into compliance. Angry that my one job as her Mummy is to protect her, and I can't. I feel angry that I didn't respond to her symptoms sooner, and angry that it wouldn't have made any difference anyway. I have failed… and God? I have never felt this type of anger around God before. I don't want to look directly at it; I just want to keep going. Lord, help.

Silence

December 2021

I was driving in the car, waiting in traffic. The three girls were in the back, playfully arguing about the right way to make a Christmas tree with their fingers and singing, 'Oh Christmas Tree'. Even though Emily is in the middle of her radiotherapy regime, here they were just being regular kids, enjoying each other and mucking around.

Suddenly, I felt out of my body. A deep howl came from my gut as I cried silently, "I want all of my children, God! Please do something!" But there was no sign or answer. There was nothing. Silence. I felt myself back in the car, blinking back tears and refocusing on the road. With the deep ache still in my chest, I kept driving. The kids kept singing in the back seat. Life, and Emily's cancer, kept going.

> Meanwhile, where is God? This is one of the most disquieting symptoms. When you are happy, so happy that you have no sense of needing Him, so happy that you are tempted to feel His claims upon you as an interruption, if you remember yourself and turn to Him with gratitude and praise, you will be – or so it feels – welcomed with open arms. But go to Him when your need is desperate, when all other help is vain, and what do you find? A door slammed in your face, and a sound of bolting and double bolting on the inside. After that, silence. You may as well turn away. The longer you wait, the more emphatic the silence will become. There are no lights in the windows. It might be an empty house. Was it ever inhabited? It seemed so once. (Lewis, p. 7)

Wordless

December 2021

I have lost access to my voice; it is too close to my soul. I cry in every song at church. I can barely listen to the talks. I blank out in the prayers. By myself, I am reading through the Psalms, but I struggle to find words to pray. My heart is stuck in a wordless grief, and I am exhausted from running to and from the hospital; always holding children. I often hear that high pitched ringing sound in my ears. I feel locked in a survival mode of silence; "I [am] too troubled to speak" (Ps. 77:4b). Every day is relentless with cancer. Watching, comforting, waiting, worrying on the sidelines.

On my first night off from looking after Em in the hospital, I couldn't sleep so I watched *The Lord of the Rings: The Two Towers* and went straight to the scene where King Theoden buries his son. At a beautiful mountainside grave, he says to Gandalf, "No parent should have to bury their child". Gandalf tries to comfort him with words of his son safe and surrounded by family in the afterlife, but Theoden breaks down and weeps. In my spirit, I showed this to the Lord. "Look Lord, this is it. Whatever words of comfort others can bring, and even though Em will go to heaven, I will still have to bury my daughter."

Pictures and scenes of loss keep coming to me now, from movies, novels, poems, or the Bible. I am so overwhelmed; I struggle for my own words or expression for this. So, I am finding the words of others, and I show them to You, Lord.

New visitor

January 2022

I have found grief made me numb initially, then angry. We're in the "waiting" period now, where hospital visits have paused, and we don't know what will happen next with Em's tumour. How long will we get with Em? And so, the grief has changed again into a deep inhale with no exhale; I'm constantly holding my breath, waiting. Grief does not seem to be one thing; it seems to visit in different ways for different times. Some parts of it feel right, and some parts of it I am struggling against.

It comes storming through my door, loud and blubbering. Or it comes shuffling in awkwardly, strong and stoic. It comes in and poses as anxiety and body aches. It comes as tiredness and brain fog. It comes as anger, or a background irritability. It comes as questions, longings, and emptiness. Most of all, it is constantly uncomfortable. Grief comes to me as that changeable visitor.

It is hard to be fully present for other people as I work around this new visitor. I try to act normal, but often I feel awkward as the silent new visitor looms beside me. It is hard to talk to you, God, in the same old ways. I find the need to draw near to You in new ways that are gentle and creative. This is a very hard road, help me to walk it with You, Lord.

Parent and child

January 2022

The harshest reality to contend with is that my love is not powerful enough to save her life. I feel like I should be strong enough to save her. Em has finally finished her radiotherapy, but what will it achieve? We are praying for a miracle, but it is gut-wrenching to walk beside her knowing I cannot stop what will probably, eventually, engulf her.

The story of our faith is also of a parent and child. The Father saw His son's slow and terrible suffering. So, was part of the meaning of the earthquakes, the darkness, the curtain torn, the dead raised – was that an All-powerful Father horrified at watching His son die? Did shaking the earth and blocking the sun vent out some of the wrongness of witnessing someone you love having to suffer so much?

Please

March 2022

We are almost five months into this cancer. Em has only had three days break in-between where the effects of radiotherapy fatigue finally wore off and this new deterioration started. Only three days of brightness and energy. One trip to the pool where she could swim almost normally. One normal day at church where she stayed in Sunday school the whole time. One great day at school. Saturday, Sunday, and Monday. Just three days of payoff for the six weeks of treatment that were so hard for her to endure. And now the tide is turning towards her final deterioration.

God, this is really unfair. We wanted more time with her with energy and brightness. More pay off for those weeks of radiotherapy torture. We are not ready for this. Please don't take her yet. But if you must take her now, let it be like her doctor says it will probably be like – that she will just fall asleep. Please don't let her suffer too much at the end. Please take her kindly home.

> Out of the depths I cry to You
> In darkest places I will call
> Incline Your ear to me anew
> And hear my cry for mercy Lord…
>
> I will wait for You, I will wait for You
> on your Word I will rely,
> I will wait for you, surely wait for you
> 'Til my soul is satisfied…
>
> I will wait for You, I will wait for You
> Through the storm and through the night
> I will wait for You, surely wait for You
> For Your love is my delight. (Getty et al., 2018)

The losses

May 2022

Cancer is slowly stripping Em of everything. The first loss was riding a bike, and realising she'd never get off training wheels. Then it was a fast succession of emergency surgeries. Then six weeks of radiotherapy. She lost being able to go to preschool altogether and was only able to go to kindergarten for an hour in the morning for one school term. She has only had two months break between active treatment and the start of this terminal progression. She had three energetic days, free of fatigue. Then the suffering really caved in on her.

On 'Mother's Day', Em woke up in 'locked in' syndrome. This means she is *not* going to die quickly in her sleep; she will be in the percentage that dies slowly and terribly. She can no longer talk, or move, or eat. She can hardly focus her eyes. She can no longer hear us. All she can do is lie and stare and wait for death. Em can only communicate to us through clumsy nodding motions when we point at pictures in a book we've made for her. She nuzzles into us for comfort or occasionally pushes us away in an attempt to express the depths of her sorrow. She cannot even cry anymore, and the release of her sadness is reduced to single drops of tears. Her humour is gone, her laugh is gone. She is trapped in her body, but death won't come.

We are seven months into this now. Eight weeks into this 'final stage'. I have begged God so many nights to take my child peacefully in her sleep, only to wake dismayed in the morning when I hear her stirring. She opens her eyes each day to stare into more suffering. Our only meaning in life now is to be present with her as she suffers. To keep letting her know that she is not alone, helping her connect to us with pictures, and comforting her. Sometimes, many times now, all we can do is hold her.

I cannot bear to think about what God is doing in this; His ways are beyond understanding. Like Job, it is better to remember my place as a human and not try to understand things that are beyond mortal reach. Like the ultimate meaning of why God would let a five-year-old suffer like this. The purpose. The point. These are questions without answers in this life. Right now, any good achieved by her suffering cannot make sense of this to me, but I cannot see all ends. I weep and submit. And I just wish this had never happened.

2

LAMENT

Reflections continuing from my experience as Emily's mother, from the time of Emily's death until the few months after her death.

… for your daughter was part of yourself; and therefore nature in you, being, as it were, cut and halved, will indeed be grieved…. (Rutherford, p. 35)

Gone

24 May 2022

The last day of Em's life involved our family shut away in a tight cocoon, completely exhausted at the finish line of cancer and death. Ten weeks into this 'final stage'. B.J. and I could hardly cry or think or move yesterday. We lay around the living room all day next to Em. B.J. woke me at 1 a.m. We sat next to her, I held her hand and he held her head. She gasped and held her breath multiple times, coming in and out of passing. B.J. asked to pray, and his prayer sent her sweetly on her way; Em finally stopped her struggle. She was finally still, at peace, *gone*. We wept. I stroked her little hand for the last time.

We arranged her in her 'nest', her special living room daybed, and pulled the blanket up to her neck: we can't pull it over her head just yet. So now she just looks like she's asleep in the living room. We lie in the sofa bed beside her and try to rest, but I can't sleep. Soon, in half an hour, I'll have to start ringing around. Start organising. The world will keep turning without her. But I already feel this deep blankness, this emptiness. I thought I would feel more relieved that she is out of suffering now, but I don't. I just feel like the sunshine in my life has been turned down, and now I must settle with a life that's dimmer.

In the early days and weeks after Emily's diagnosis, it was hard to find sleep or words or a way up. But at least I had Emily's suffering to give me a reason to hold it together. She needed me day and night for seven months. But now she has died, there is nothing. No cancer to fight. No symptoms to alleviate. No brow to stroke. No hand to hold. Nothing to hold back the grief that has been waiting for me. Thick, heavy, suffocating. The months of bracing now followed by a feeling of drowning.

Part of me feels scared of forgetting who she was. That we already lost her so slowly over so many months, and that may have blunted our grief. Will we honour her in our grief? Will we remember her?

But then I picture her in a memory: all the many mornings she climbed into my bed for a snuggle with me. Pretending our fingers were animals together. Talking about her many random thoughts. Then the pain of her loss is like my heart has cracked in two, and I don't know how I will keep going after her. How could I forget her? How do I live with all these memories of her?

> Have mercy on me, my God, have mercy on me,
> for in you I take refuge.
> I will take refuge in the shadow of your wings
> until the disaster has passed (Ps. 57:1).

Buried

June 2022

> In a way that is different from every other human relationship, a child is bone of his parents' bone, flesh of their flesh. When a child dies, part of the parents is buried. (Bayly, p. 65)
>
> I buried myself that warm June day. (Wolterstorff, p. 42)

Love is safe

June 2022
We are bunkered down after the funeral services now, many of us sick. I can feel my body finally giving way to months of fatigue, and fever is making my grief more vivid. I keep seeing Em today as she came to me two months ago. That time I was napping on my bed, and she came and put her arm around me and napped with me. The memory of her simple gesture of love now hangs heavy on me as longing. I am longing to hold her.

Longings and hauntings. I'm also haunted by the thought that the suffering Em went through may have meant she could not feel my love at the end, or that any mistakes I may have made as a mother will have outweighed the love that I gave her. Or maybe the years ahead will alter me into someone she doesn't recognise. Part of me fears seeing her in heaven, after maybe decades apart, that maybe it will not be the meeting I now hope for. Will this love between us still be held safe?

But then I keep remembering Em climbing into my bed and freely offering me her cuddles. I have thought of 1 Corinthians 13 – that all else will pass away, but the greatest, everlasting element is love. Love must be able to survive these many long years of separation, and love will last into eternity. Like the old hymn, "I know whom I have believed and am persuaded that He is able to keep that which I've committed unto Him until that Day". Our mother-daughter love is now a very great thing I am committing to God for what may be the long decades ahead.

The Hole

June 2022

There is a hole in our family now that we are all trying to live around. The brutal part is that we must keep on living. During family devotions last night, L. told us that every night since Emily died, she has been praying for the end of all things so that we can all be together as a family again. B.J. and I had tears streaming down our faces because we now long for the end too, but we know it may not happen that way. Instead, it may be many decades before we see Em again, and our long lives now stretch before us without her.

Our family must go on without her, with this gaping hole in it now. We all know we are less without her here. She was the quirky one, the funny one, the independent one. We've lost that now, and all her life's potential is gone. Home does not feel the same anymore. Home is uncomfortable. Grief is uncomfortable. You cannot get away from it; it follows you around, like a weight tied to your leg.

You cannot go to where she is, and each passing day takes you further away from her time on this earth. Her earthly life is now relegated to the past. Her presence will be reduced to a carefully curated bunch of her photos and treasured belongings. These memorials of her cannot hug us or laugh with us or talk with us. They stay forever the same, and yet we must change. We try to imagine what she would have said, or preferred in a situation, but our imaginings are pale. Her sisters will grow up without her now. We will change this house, our jobs, our lives; we will work, laugh, love, and live. We will keep going on this earth without her. We must keep going.

You have left in my heart
A hole as wide
As the world, my child,
And as long as the rest of my life.
(McKelvey, p. 177)

Clothes

June 2022

I am sitting in the grief. I started organising her clothes today and just wept my way through unloading her little closet. Sobbing through the underwear and socks and swimmers and uniforms and pyjamas and clothes. I cried as I sorted it carefully into what to keep for a memory quilt I will have made, what to just keep, what to give away, and what is too worn out to do anything with. It feels like I've been holding it together for seven months and now it is time to just weep. To sit in the sadness. She is gone, and now I must slowly start to pack up her life.

This morning, I read Psalm 63:7: "Because you are my help, I sing in the shadow of your wings." Again, in Psalm 91:4: "He will cover you with his feathers, and under his wings you will find refuge…" The same picture is in Psalm 17:8 and 36:7. That God sees us as little chicks to be held in at His side, under His wing. If God is the Mother Hen in this picture, then Em is under one wing in heaven, and we are here on earth under the other wing. A divide is between us. One day, at the end of all things, both wings will unite. For now, though, we are separated chicks under our different wings, and Divine love is covering us both.

After careful sorting, I washed Em's clothes on a delicate cycle, using a sensitive laundry powder. I hung both loads out on the washing line with care, taking my time. They hang there now in the winter breeze, an unnatural grouping of just 'her'. No longer blended into the family's huge pile of daily clothes, but separate and special and fleeting. This will be the last time Em's clothes all hang on the clothesline. They flap around in the cold sunshine, waving goodbye.

Pruned

June 2022

I stared blankly at only two lunch boxes this morning. I'd instinctively started looking for the third, and then had to stop myself. Often, and yet still unexpectedly, that sharp snap back to our new reality happens in these everyday moments: only two lunch boxes now, only four plates needed at dinner now, only four piles of laundry now. Then I must remember all over again; she is gone.

A lot of my roles were bound up with her. She was the last of my babies; she was the longest in my arms. As the youngest, when the older two were at school, she spent a lot of her week with me. Then she became sick, so we spent all our days and nights with her. I helped carry her everywhere. I shadowed her at school. I was her craft companion, and her confidant. I was often the one she came to for comfort and hugs. At the end, alongside B.J., I was her palliative care team at home.

Her life was wound so tightly around my own, and then she left.

Tending the soul

July 2022

Sometimes I can feel philosophical about her loss, but at other times it is all ugliness. I visited her gravesite yesterday and an angry emptiness hit me as I sorted my flower arrangement over the freshly pressed earth, "this is all my relationship with Em is now in this life: tending her grave". I shoved the feelings away, but they came back at 3 a.m. this morning as I awoke in tears.

In my deepest parts, a now well-worn mourning cry is aching in me, "I want my daughter back". B.J. and I sometimes talk of how part of us wants to die to go and be with her. I have trouble looking at children her age or families with three children. I feel cut off from that now, I feel jealous of it, and I want my old life back. Late at night, or in the early morning, the ugliness of her loss can hit.

In those moments, it's hard to know how to tend my soul; to balance grief and avoid bitterness. Sometimes I feel swept up in a deep urge to cry, as though tears have been hanging over me for a time and must find a release. I instinctively let the dam burst and sit in the sadness. I honour her loss.

But sometimes I feel a need to fight the ugliness and claim back my own life. I tell myself that jealousy of others is pointless. At times Frankl's insights are helpful, "no man and no destiny can be compared with any other man or any other destiny" (Frankl, p. 85). This situation is happening, and therefore it is given by God and *must* have meaning – rather than some vision of my life as I think it should be. I also remind myself that she was not, in fact, *my* baby. She was always God's, and I only had "lease" of her (Rutherford, p. 13). That I cannot let grief over one child overwhelm me because I still have two other children to raise. To love. To be present for.

But I am not always certain how to tend my soul. Sometimes I just feel lost.

Memorial

July 2022

A month after she had gone, and the sorting of her belongings had ground to a halt. Her toys, clothes, favourite pair of shoes, her craft… all of it had been corralled around and under her desk. It stayed safely huddled there so we could move through the rest of the house without accidentally wrecking a memory of her. Her desk was a special place to her, and she spent hours organising and rearranging her knick-knacks inside of it. I could not disturb this last piece of her yet, but her mess of possessions was frozen all over it.

Now her sisters have decided we should build an 'Elephant House' for her favourite things, so they can be looked at, enjoyed, and carefully played with. So, we're slowly getting a display shelf together for it. I am tearfully sorting through her desk and enjoying each little treasure. It is a gradual process to reorganise the little life she built and honour her flexibly in the house.

> She died, and left to me
> This heath, this calm and quiet scene;
> The memory of what has been,
> And never more will be.
> (Wordsworth, 1798)

Quiet myself

July 2022

How hard it is to send my child where I could not go before her. Every day since she passed away, I see Em in the same scene in my mind, close to her death. She was lying next to me on the couch at the end of the day. She snuggled into my side and flung her weak arm over my body, "Mummy, when I die, I will miss your huggles in heaven". Now every day I hear her voice in my head across the great divide and it aches deep in my heart, "Mummy… I will miss your huggles in heaven…"

I try to quiet my heart, and trust that the reasons for Em leaving us must be very good, far outweighing the possible reasons for her remaining with us (Romans 8:28). Emily must see more of those reasons now in heaven; those great interweaving answers for all the many questions and longings we have here. She must know more of why she had to suffer and die, and she will be comforted by God Himself (Rev 21:4). I am trusting that my beautiful daughter is at peace (Isa. 57:2). So, I will quiet myself in that.

> And now they live and dwell within
> your glorious love and light,
> vibrant and hale and satisfied in you.
> (McKelvey, p. 191)

3

LOSS IN MARRIAGE

Reflections centring around how Emily's story impacted my marriage, from the time of Emily's diagnosis until the few months after her death.

O God! Can I not grasp
Them with a tighter clasp?
O God! Can I not save
One from the pitiless wave?
(Poe, 1849)

Suddenly

November 2021

Within two days of Emily's terminal diagnosis, B.J. and I sat on the farthest park bench in the gardens at the children's hospital while Emily was in her first surgery. We kept saying to each other, "Is this a dream? Is this actually happening?" The whole thing feels like a nightmare. Like a ship, our lives have overturned in this storm, and everything on deck has been sent flying.

We didn't have a lot of time, so we quickly discussed the most pressing logistics for dropping everything to care for Em. I had already quit my job and paused my university studies. B.J. was about to take a huge leave of absence from work, which would delay completion of his specialist training and leave us living off savings and annual leave. After years of planning our big move to the coast, we decided within minutes to halt the move. We would stay in our current home. It was the only home Emily had ever known, and we couldn't uproot her now. We even talked about whether we would ever have more children.

We were bringing up huge topics and making decisions on them in a matter of minutes, trying to quell our panic by nailing down any resolution. The biggest topic we kept circling back to was Em. *We are going to lose a child sometime in the next year.* We could not wrap our heads around this, and there was no decision or sacrifice we could make to change the outcome. We were dazed and gripped tightly on to each other.

Space

November 2021
After the initial terrible news about Emily was broken to us, B.J. and I were almost immediately taken in to see Emily in the large multi-bed theatre recovery room and told to wait by her bedside as she slept. There were multiple nurses and doctors walking around, and other patients nearby. I huddled in a corner of the busy room and called my parents and sister to tell them the news. I stifled my reaction to their cries on the end of the phone, looking at all the strangers around me.

That is hospital life; being encircled. B.J. and I take turns each day going to and from the hospital with Em. We stand by helplessly as health professionals turn up at Em's bedside, often randomly, for observations or procedures or consultations. We're on their schedule; in their space. At home it's a lot better, but space is still warped. Visitors turn up to our house at all hours, sometimes unannounced. Family and friends have also travelled from great distances to come see us. So, we now have more people in our home but less energy than usual to host them.

The night of the diagnosis, B.J. stayed with Emily in hospital, and I returned to my car to go home to the two older girls. Before starting the car, I sat in the dark silence for a few minutes, shaking. I was finally alone. Over the next few days, I've added to my short list of private spaces: the laundry room, the garage, the clothesline, and the shower.

In the hospital, we also often go to the gardens with Em. These spaces are away from everyone, and we can finally stop for a few minutes. Sit in the silence. The rest of the time, we often feel as though we are surrounded.

Help

November 2021

We've said 'yes' to every meal, every gift, and every bit of help in these first few weeks. We are in a daze of going daily to and from the hospital, but we have slowly regretted saying 'yes' to everyone. We have people turning up to our door frequently and sometimes randomly, and we can barely shut our fridge or freezer from all the food. Last night it was overwhelming – we were given a meal for about thirty people when there is only five of us, and Emily is so sick she couldn't eat any of it. I gaped at the feast and felt immediately how we need to snap out of this survival-mode stupor. *We have to manage our lives again.*

Yet it is also in these out-of-control help situations that we are unexpectedly blessed. Em's appetite is faded and changeable now due to the tumour, and it is hard to predict what she will eat. One night, after another day at the hospital, we were expecting an unknown meal drop off from one of the older ladies from church. Em looked at the door expectantly, "Mummy, I hope it's custard for dinner".

I replied, "Em, I have no idea what's coming. But let's pray right now that it is custard."

We prayed together. We opened our front door. It was custard.

Time

December 2021

Organising time between extended family, friends, and immediate family feels very pressured now. B.J. and I sit down in the backyard with our calendars open at the start of every week and portion out our free time between both sides of the family, our friends, and then some time for just our family of five. There are a lot of competing demands. Everyone feels time with our Em slipping between their fingers, and everyone wants one more special moment with her. Some of our families have made a big effort to visit from hours away, interstate or overseas.

Yet we are also exhausted. Em herself does not feel well and is a shy character. Having realistic expectations, clear communication and even picking the right activity to do together so that Em can enjoy herself takes a lot of preplanning. At the start of each week, B.J. and I carve out the calendar and take wearied turns suggesting compromises. It is exhausting to plan out what's left of Em's life.

Finding each other

December 2021

Each day B.J. and I are either driving Em in and out of the hospital for treatment or looking after our other children. By the time we reconnect at the end of the day we are still surrounded by children who want to cling onto us to sleep. We are in an autopilot survival mode.

Our baby is slowly dying. We are giving each other a wide berth, each aware that the other is either flung out under another grief wave; or silent and grim in the in-between, recovering. We have only once broken down in tears at the same time together. Most of the time we are tag teaming the grief; as I resurface, he goes under.

Or as it was this morning, we were both drunken in our own separate grief and unable to reach each other. B.J. wanted a hug and I wanted to be left alone; I often feel I have nothing left to give him. The other day, a nurse tried to encourage me to do something for my own leisure, and I sat there blankly trying to think of what I used to enjoy for myself. I have nothing left for myself; I am almost completely absorbed in the 'mother' role now.

It was late afternoon and I stared blankly at B.J., exhausted. The children chattered away in the background, accentuating the huge gulf between us. We sat together and held hands and talked in low voices about finding each other. Neither of us had any answers but we wanted to keep finding each other.

Weaknesses

February 2021

B.J. and I are having a lot more arguments since Emily's diagnosis. I can stumble into arguments when I think I'm about to have a simple conversation. Or I can wait in readiness for them because I feel owed. Arguments when we're both exhausted, and one of us just seems to be asking the other to do one more chore. Arguments about who has invited another visitor over without warning. Arguments when one of us needs to talk or hug but the other is too exhausted. Arguments about finances, and our sudden change in them. Arguments about sleep, and who was getting more of it.

A child slowly dying in a household creates a lot of stress. Stress is laying down landmines for arguments that we are sometimes tripping over unawares, and sometimes setting off deliberately. Sometimes we try to name the stress or the fault and apologise explicitly. Or sometimes we just look at each other exhausted, and we know it's not worth the words; just drop it.

Us

May 2022

There are many moments of Emily's suffering, and now her slow dying, that only B.J. and I will see. We look at each other, or squeeze each other's hand, and we know what the other is thinking. We try to fill in the gaps for each other, but we can be very different witnesses sometimes.

B.J. wears his heart more on his sleeve, whereas I am often more stoic. In our grieving, he has struggled more with disbelief, and I more with anger. He wants to talk and hold me close; I want to be quiet and get on with the job. As a mother, I am constantly holding Em and managing the older girls; and I also prepared a cemetery that would allow for a family plot. As an OT, I predominantly organised the furniture and equipment in our home to be appropriate for Emily at the end. For the hospital at home set-up and cemetery discussions, B.J. just burst into tears.

Yet, as a doctor, B.J. is calm and clear-headed through Em's many medical procedures that I can't bear to watch. He is now syringing liquified food down the back of Emily's throat while I cower in another room, wringing my hands. He has had to do unbelievable things as Emily's Daddy/ doctor: manage her tube feeding; organise and administer her around the clock medications. Our marriage has never been to such a dark place as this, and we have never needed each other in these ways before.

Desperate

May 2022

We are both desperate to save her. Em is in her final days and hours at home, lying unconsciously in her special "nest" bed in the living room. B.J. and I are her palliative care team, nursing her through the days and nights, and we are struggling.

B.J. cannot stand to watch her fading. As a doctor, he is wracked by not actively intervening: by not feeding her diminishing body and instead watching her grow thinner, her ribs now sticking out. He wants to actively assist her breathing. Everything in him wants to revive her. He wants to save her life.

I cannot stand to watch her suffer anymore. Everything in me wants her to go in peace. I do not want to revive her. I want her to let go of this wretched life. I want to save her from this life.

We are sometimes arguing and sometimes agreeing about how much to intervene, versus accepting that she is dying, and letting her go. There is no one else here with us to make these decisions in the early hours, it's just he and I doing this at home. Both of us exhausted. Both of us desperate.

Bearing witness

June 2022

In the initial weeks after Em's death, B.J. and I were together at home in the grieving. We walked in nature together, we talked of Em together, we cried together. Now B.J. is back to full-time work, busy in a hectic workplace and surrounded by colleagues. I am working from home, in a now very quiet house, walking past reminders of Em everywhere. We now hold it together and let go into the grief at different times, in different ways. We talk about the change and disorientation of trying to live 'normally' again, with Em's loss always on the edges.

Going through losing a child in our marriage has sometimes been a shared experience and has sometimes been isolating. We are alone, together. We grieve from our unique perspective as 'Mummy' or 'Daddy'. Only we can fully know the sorrow in that role, and the private memories, hopes and dreams that will be mourned. We walk our grief at a different pace.

Then there is the shared 'parent' grief that we hold onto together. Even though we have a different angle on it, we alone share it for the other. So many moments of Emily's birth, her life, her strengths, her suffering, her questionings, her joys, her tears and even her death were only witnessed by us two together. We have become the principal keepers of those memories, and our love for Em, for each other.

4

GOODBYE BETWEEN SISTERS

Reflections on my observations of our two older daughters (six years old and eight years old) from the time of Emily's diagnosis until the few months after her death.

Who was it, when we both were young,
First prais'd me with her artless tongue,
And on my neck delighted hung?
My Sister.

For we would run about all day,
And when at hide-and-seek we'd play,
Who came to find me where I lay?
My Sister.
(Taylor, 1782–1866)

Sister-grief

November 2021

A few weeks after Em's diagnosis, L. volunteered to pray for the first time at family devotions. She prayed that Emily would be healed. Long after bedtime, L. came into my bedroom and broke down crying. After I soothed her, she finally went to bed looking peaceful, but that look is transient. Instead, she now often looks stressed. Where she used to have reserve, she is now snappier and brittle. She looks like a kid who is trying to hold it together.

In contrast, D. seems to be deliberately uncurious about Emily's situation. Her focus is, "Em is ok *today*". She often rounds off questions like she is rounding off the issue in her mind, smoothing off any loose thoughts. Still, some loose thoughts are troubling her. She tells me of new tummy pains, then headaches, her hair is bothering her more, and now her clothes feel more "annoying".

One month after Em's diagnosis, it has all caught up with her. D. found me this evening and couldn't stop crying. The tummy pain was not stopping. She felt sick but she didn't understand why or where. D. just sobbed and sobbed. I hugged her, and we lay huddled together on a mattress in the living room. Soon I had D. on one side of me sobbing, Emily on the other side holding my hand, and L. lying above my head. All three kids holding onto me. After half an hour of us cuddled together, the girls slowly calmed down. I then peeled away to be alone, now distraught; their sister-grief can be overwhelming to witness.

It

January 2022

It's been three months since Em's diagnosis. Over that time, we have not found a way to talk as a family about Emily's possible death directly yet. We've been helping the older girls manage their stress symptoms, but we were not ready to face the cause with them. Then late into the evening last night, both older girls appeared at the living room door. L. said she was worried that Emily might pass away, and she couldn't sleep. We all sat on our fold-out couch, L. was teary, and D. sat next to her trying to comfort her. I started to talk, but my throat was closing over, and I was faltering. B.J. took over:

"Girls, it's time we talk about *it* with you".

He summarised the situation we faced: "Em has finished treatment for now and her sickness in the brain is the same size. She is tired, but one day that might change. If she gets sicker and passes away, it will probably not happen very suddenly so we will have time to get ready for it. It is perfectly normal to feel worried, and to cry about what is happening to Em. We have a lot of people around us who are supporting us. We are praying for a miracle, but we don't know if that will happen. If Em dies, we know she will be safe in heaven. We will all be together in heaven again one day. But this is very hard to accept. In the meantime, we are trying to have special memories together. We want to enjoy you all together, and especially enjoy Emily."

D. had started off trying to offer her own consoling amongst B.J.'s speech, but B.J. soon asked her to just listen. She looked at me, helpless and hurt, now exposed to the full bleak message. B.J. and L. wept throughout, and soon I joined their tears. I felt D. looking up at me in worry. As we prayed together and said "Amen", D. finally let her guard down and wept into my lap. We all held onto each other; all four of us were together in *it* now.

> They had gone forth together into their new life of sorrow, and they would never more see the sunshine undimmed by remembered cares. (Eliot, p. 171)

Play evolving

February 2022

The girls show us what they need to connect with each other, now that Emily is weaker. We often must carry Em around outdoors, and she naps frequently, so she now struggles at school, at playgrounds and in the outside world. But inside our house is her safe place. So now the big rollicking backyard games the girls used to play have simply moved indoors. Jumping on the trampoline has changed to flopping onto the couch together. Park adventures are now playmat adventures. The girls continue to muck around, laugh, imagine, and create together. They often move as a single entity, playing off each other's energy. They bicker at times, but they have instinctively known how to adapt their play for Em without needing to say a word.

Emily and D. spent two hours yesterday playing in "Toyville" together on the playmat, renovating their toy character's houses, making up songs and games for the toys.

They had a "Funder Wonder Festival" for their toys, and there were arch enemies who created problems throughout. Emily had energy the whole time for playing and wasn't left out of it once. They sat together and chatted, made voices for their toys, and brought their shared world to life.

Big sisters

April 2022

There are many times that B.J. and I are lost in the bigger picture of what is happening, and the older two girls help us. Like when Emily's breathing was deteriorating rapidly, and we were trying to fly her home from her final "Make A Wish" holiday. B.J. and I were silent and tense on the plane, as Emily heaved loudly, struggling for breath. We were not sure if Emily would make it through the flight. In that anxious moment, L. decided to pull out one of her musical birthday cards and announced, "it's time!". We all cracked up laughing with the ridiculous tune whining across the back seats of the plane. Em cackled, and the tension was lifted a little.

The girls constantly have a whirlwind of jokes happening, and even when Emily can hardly find breath to join in, they let the jokes roll on. Emily's once deep chuckle, now a pale hack of its former self, still rings out. We see the older girls' kindness, in giving Emily the prime position in games or in front of books or in bringing her toys to her. D. patiently stands at the TV and points out the options so Emily can pick all her favourites shows. There are so many moments the older girls are being asked to be second now and they are stepping up and doing it. They are shouldering so much as big sisters.

God answered "no"

May 2022

As Em can no longer swallow and will need a feeding tube inserted at the hospital, we sat around for family devotions last night to discuss it with all three girls. Em lay next to us, frail and quiet, and we all huddled around her. Em's body is slowly shutting down, and she can no longer hear anything either. So, we used our hands clasped together in prayer to motion to her that we were praying for her.

B.J. and I broke down in front of the girls while we were praying for Em. We've never done that before; both sobbed at the same time in front of the girls. We tried to pray hopefully but we are heartbroken. As soon as we said "Amen", both L. and D. then went away to their bedroom, sobbing. As B.J. stayed with Em in the living room, I prepared both the older girls heat packs and then sat quietly with them. After she calmed down enough to speak, L. said to me, "So, God's answer to all our prayers for a miracle is 'no'. He won't help Emily. I don't understand why He would do this to Emily. I don't understand why He would do this to us." D. added with a sob, "I can't stand seeing Emily so sick".

We all cried deeply, huddled together. I told them that I felt the same as them, and that I didn't understand it. I talked about how we won't have complete answers for why Em is suffering in this life. But we trust that there is something amazing waiting for Emily, and she will be safe and happy in heaven soon. For now, all we can do is be with her as she suffers so she is not alone. So that she knows we see her and what she's going through, and that we love her.

Slowly the girls calmed down. They talked of Emily finally happy in heaven.

Slow goodbye

May 2022

In the month before her passing, Emily retreated into herself as her suffering increased. She clung to B.J. and I but pulled back from her sisters. Maybe to her they represented 'fun' and 'play'; all the things she was being cut off from now. Her sickness gave her little reserve for being with them, so she could be short tempered. L. and D. were upset at first when they saw her pushing away their hugs. Their service to her became setting up the TV for her or playing a video game for her to watch. They became her companions at a distance, and Em turned inwards.

The older girls then had a lot of time playing alone, just the two of them, while B.J. and I cared for Emily by ourselves at the end. This unexpectedly went on for a few weeks. By the time Emily finally passed away, the older girls told us that they felt like she had passed away "a while ago". Cancer has taken Emily away from her sisters in pieces. They've now entered life without Em by slow degrees, like the change of a season.

Play again

June 2022

Play has changed for the older two girls. On the surface things look similar, but underneath their play has cracks and patch-ups. Tears come up for the girls in unexpected places while they try to retrace their old play together:

"She's not playing the game the way Emily used to. Emily's not *here* anymore."

"We can't play 'Neighbours' or 'Builders'; this is the first time since Emily…"

Or like this morning, visits to the park are shorter, and the two girls are more weary. Once we arrived home, L. unusually went and lay down. D. turned to me, "Mum, can I play with you?" She would normally have paired off with Em, but now I'm often the poor substitute. Both L. and D. now burst into tears over small things that normally wouldn't bother them; today it was not understanding a new board game and not wearing warm enough clothes for the park. Games that were previously easy now take more concentration, and they bickered at each other when a simple Lego construction went wrong today.

But there are also new repairs. Initially, "Toyville" was shut down for the month after Emily passed away. Last week, the girls decided to rebuild "Toyville". They told me that Emily, one of its "bosses", is now "on holidays". They restarted playing hesitantly, asking for my help to get going, as "Emily usually had the ideas and did the voices". After a couple of hours, they had relaxed into it. They chattered together about how the houses will work now, and what the latest Toy festival competitions will be. For a little while, the energy between them was carefree and fun again.

The cost

July 2022

How do I begin to count the cost for my two older daughters? The first week after Emily had passed away, both older girls came to us and told us of problems they'd been having at school all year, but that they'd been shielding us from:

"It might take us a while to realise that we can come to you for help again. For a long time, we could only come to you with really big problems and the rest, we had to figure it out… it will take us a while to come to you again for help".

"I couldn't tell you what was going on when Emily was here."

Now five weeks since Em left us, and the girls struggle in different ways at school. Both feel over-sensitive in the playground now. One is struggling because the boys around her in her class keep playing games involving mock dying, like, "I got you – you're dead now", and she cannot cope with hearing kids joking about dying. One is struggling because of the large playground groups; she prefers everything quieter at the moment.

I sit with the girls after school, and we listen to them in family devotions every night. Their surface stories change every day, but the underlying story is always the same – *The three of them is now two.*

Memory keeping play

July 2022

Saturday morning runs at a slow pace in our house, and it is also the start of the school holidays. The two older girls decide that Emily's beloved toy elephants need to be freshened up, and so they set up an 'Elephant salon' for them in the living room. Emily had a large assortment of treasured elephants, and they are carefully being lined up to be brushed and have hairclips put on their ears.

Emily's most loyal companion elephant "Ellie" is wheeled around the house on Emily's office chair to survey the scene and is given tour guide commentary. Ellie needs rearranging, so the two girls work together to lift her up, and carefully lay out Emily's blanket for her so that she will be comfortable. The sisters play tenderly in their memories of Em.

> Oh, my sister, passing from me,
> Out of human care and strife,
> Leave me, as a gift, those virtues
> Which have beautified your life…
> Henceforth, safe across the river
> I shall see forever more
> A beloved household spirit
> Waiting for me on the shore….
> (Alcott, p. 394)

5

SORROW WITHIN COMMUNITY

Reflections centring around our interactions with our wider community, from the time of Emily's diagnosis until the few months after her passing.

Then [Job's three friends] sat on the ground with him
for seven days and seven nights.
No one said a word to him, because they saw how
great his suffering was.
(Job 2:13)

Communication

November 2021

In these weeks of daily radiotherapy, the support from our family, friends, the church, the school, our workplaces – everyone has been incredible, and overwhelming. We have so many people contacting us and wanting updates about Emily's daily cancer treatment. Everyone wants to know how we are. We must also contact so many people to reorganise our lives quickly. We have set up a group update, but we are still swamped in communication. When people ask us generally, "is there anything you need?" we have no idea what to say. We appreciate the warm sentiment, but we are blank. I have started to love the "you don't have to reply" support messages. I feel numb looking down at my phone and seeing more and more unanswered messages. We are so weary.

Human effort will beat this cancer

December 2021

Having a child who is being treated for terminal cancer, I am now getting a lot of unsolicited health advice. Comments like "Many people go overseas for treatment", "Have we tried this new drug?", "What diet is Emily on?", "Have we done our research?", "Have we got a second opinion?", "Positive thoughts will change the outcome", "Emily is strong and she will beat the cancer", "It will be ok" or "She's a fighter".

I am often told stories of people who have defied the medical odds and lived passed their terminal diagnosis 'used by date'. Acquaintances send me the names of treatments that might be promising. My sister even got offered the details of a strict diet and some expensive machine which 'heals' cancer.

I know these people mean well, but they are also inadvertently sending me the message that Emily *has to* live, and it is up to *me* to make that happen. I don't think they realise that I am already facing a daily battle with doubt and guilt. We are stuck inside the ultimate decision-making labyrinth, fighting for the life of our child. Every day we face difficult treatment choices, we regret missing symptoms, and we agonise over whether we are doing our very best. We are already working, researching, advice asking and praying harder than we have ever done before.

But ultimately, choices in terminal cancer feel like an illusion.

Faith will beat this cancer

January 2022

Hardest of all are the few people who are expecting healing for Emily. That fasting or faith will heal her. That a miracle is coming for her. Even being told by people that they are praying solely for a miracle is difficult. I wish they also had prayers for how we will handle the other, more likely, outcome.

A few trusted people in my life have sent me the same story from Daniel 3 – Shadrach, Meshach, and Abednego.

In this story, these men faced an impossible situation. They saw both life and death as possible outcomes, but they still trusted God regardless. And in the furnace, God was there with them. So, this is how we are trying to pray. We are praying for a miracle, as Em is daily asking us to do, but we are also praying to accept whatever happens. We are trying to hold both hope and submission in our prayers, and to trust that God is with us in this suffering.

Humility

February 2022

"What do you think Emily needs?"

During almost every conversation I have with Emily's school teachers; this is the question I am asked. Like this morning, as I waited at the school for Em to finish her morning of kindergarten, this is what her teacher asked me. It has touched me deeply how humble this question is. Em's teachers are constantly open to listening, and Em's needs are front and centre for them.

Reaching out

March 2022

So many people have reached out to us during this time, in so many creative ways. Even when I am awkward and irritable and exhausted, they reach out anyway. Some have travelled long distances and dropped everything just to be near to us. Some have dropped around meals. Some have thought of meaningful gifts or experiences for Emily and the kids. Some have sent us books. Some are raising money for cancer research. Some have told us their own stories of grief. Some have just hugged us. Some have cried with us. Some ring us or message us regularly. Some pray with us regularly.

Some people are natural with us, and some people are hesitant. But we understand the cautious, "I don't know what to say" and see the love underneath it. B.J. and I often talk about these moments together; we appreciate every time someone reaches out to us.

Being with suffering

June 2022

> I was sitting, torn by grief. Someone came and talked to me of God's dealings, of why it happened, of hope beyond the grave. He talked constantly, he said things I knew were true. I was unmoved, except to wish he'd go away. He finally did.
>
> Another came and sat beside me. He didn't talk. He didn't ask leading questions. He just sat beside me for an hour and more, listened when I said something, answered briefly, prayed simply, left. I was moved. I was comforted. I hated to see him go. (Bayly, pp. 55-56)

> What I need to hear from you is that you recognise how painful it is. I need to hear from you that you are with me in my desperation. To comfort me, you have to come close. Come sit beside me on my mourning bench. (Wolterstorff, p. 34)

Arm's length

July 2022

Suffering is awkward and maybe everyone must make their private peace with it. I can sense the people who are uncomfortable or unfamiliar with suffering. Some people have a pained look when they see our family now. Or others may ask me how I am, but their expression is high pitched and bubbly, begging me for a positive reply.

When Em was alive, at times I would show tears or struggle, and there were some people who immediately plastered me in positivity – "you'll be ok", "she'll be ok", or "you have to make the most of the time". Or now, just weeks after Em has died, I sometimes get the "at least" comments, like "at least she's out of suffering now", or "at least you had five years with her". Sometimes I get the religious plastering too, like "God will use her suffering", "God must know that you were strong enough to handle this", or "You'll see her in heaven again soon".

I know, for some, seeing our sadness makes them uncomfortable and they keep me at arm's length. Maybe suffering has not been made their acquaintance yet. I can understand, but I also feel their distance.

Presence

July 2022

A comforting presence with few words is such a valuable gift when you are mourning. The friends and family who don't feel the need to say much to me: who can just sit with me as I cry. Or hold my hand for even a few seconds. The people who hurt with us. These simple moments mean the most to me – when our spirits are quiet and present with each other. There is no whitewashing of the pain; it is just allowed to be, and it is enveloped in their love.

Community

July 2022

I find crowds harder now, since Em has passed. I often stand on the periphery and feel awkward when I see happy groups huddled together. Yet at the edges of the group, a strange community has come to find me – the community of those who have lost someone close and irreplicable. They often seek me out on the edges of the sporting field, or the back of the hall, or at the farthest table. They look at me in earnest or with eyes cast down:

"I lost a child too..."

"My brother passed away when I was young..."

"My mother died last year..."

Then we stare at each other and nothing else needs to be said. Just stricken faces and tear-filled eyes, and all the polite walls that were once there have gone. Sometimes we hold each other's hand, and sometimes we just nod. We are now connected by shared stories of loss;

> ... the Father of compassion and the God of all comfort, who comforts us in all our troubles, so that we can comfort those in any trouble with the comfort we ourselves receive from God (2 Cor. 1:3-4).

6

SUFFERING AND HEALTHCARE

Reflections focusing on our interactions with health professionals, primarily in the hospital setting, from the time of Emily's diagnosis until just prior to her death.

What tormented Ivan Ilych most was the deception, the lie, which for some reason they all accepted, that he was not dying but was simply ill, and that he only need keep quiet and undergo a treatment and then something very good would result.
(Tolstoy, p. 59)

Family at the centre

October 2021

I was staying overnight with Emily at the children's hospital, lying next to her in the hospital bed. There was one nurse who came to get observations and give multiple medicines in the early hours of the morning. Everything was dark, and the only light was from the many monitors flashing and beeping around us in the four-bed ward. This nurse didn't come in around the curtain with a cheery "hi!" like most; she came in quietly. Instead of addressing Emily, she looked at me and softly told me what she was there to do. She asked if I could help prepare Emily for it, then she calmly waited for me to do my work. Emily was asleep, and so being woken up for the grim task of swallowing multiple foul-tasting medicines was upsetting. Emily woke up, looked up at the nurse and me helplessly, and then started to protest and cry.

This nurse waited patiently for me to soothe Emily; she didn't say a word. Where other nurses often stepped in and tried to be the co-mother with me at this point, this nurse let me calm Emily by myself. The nurse quietly asked me to tell her when I thought Emily was ready. This was a slow and uncertain process, and I think we slowed her down in her nursing duties by about ten minutes. But this nurse calmly waited at the bedside and worked at Emily's pace. Em finally took all her medicines, and the nurse left us quietly, without further comment. I am filled with admiration for her. This gentle nurse was sensitive to Em's suffering and her primary need for me, and she quietly worked her nursing duties around us.

Play

November 2021
In the last six days, both B.J. and I have either been in hospital with Emily non-stop, or with our other two daughters steadying them. We have barely slept or eaten or seen each other. We are getting ready for Em to have her second surgery. We have already sat through multiple long multidisciplinary conversations about her terminal diagnosis and palliative treatment, full of medical jargon upon medical jargon.

Today, B.J. and I came to the radiotherapy centre after a forty-five-minute drive through traffic. In contrast to our haggard states, the doctor who greeted us was bright and chipper. We were solemn in return, but she didn't seem to notice. She started her tour by talking about how Emily would eventually have a great time at radiotherapy. Em can "play on the huge radiotherapy machine", and "by the last weeks of treatment she will be skipping in and out of the centre". Emily can "work with a play therapist if we want". Everything about radiotherapy was made to sound fun.

We did not feel ready for the fun that was on offer. Finally, we were shown the huge radiotherapy machine. Buttons and lights flashed, and an enormous beam loomed over the tiny patient bed underneath. I stood in the room in stunned silence; it was a nightmare. The doctor continued to chatter on in the background happily about how many kids love playing in this room. Apparently as a child, Emily was expected to be playful, and we as her parents were expected to be optimistic. Any other reactions to terminal cancer, like shock or grief, had no space for expression there.

I stopped listening. All I felt was anger, so I said nothing. I hid behind my COVID mask, gripped B.J.'s hand and let him lead me out of there.

Building rapport

November 2021

We are a month into the daily radiotherapy treatments. Yesterday we'd left the house at 6:30 a.m. and had radiotherapy at 7:30 a.m. From 8:30-11 a.m., I sat at Emily's bedside as she slept after radiotherapy. She usually wakes in fits and starts, looking annoyed. She is hard to look after and appears to be having headaches or some other pain – it's hard to know. Emily partly woke up at 11 a.m., and we had to go to weekly clinic at the other hospital which is ten minutes' walk away. Emily was groggy and unable to walk but refused to get into her stroller. I insisted as I could not physically carry her that far. She finally consented, but grouched loudly for half the way there, still exhausted.

We made it to the packed clinic waiting room, and Emily slumped into the chair next to me, closing her eyes to sleep. Unfortunately, as the hour ticked by, we kept being spotted by cheery health professionals. In total, seven health professionals came by: three play therapists, two nurses, and two allied health professionals. None of them explicitly asked my permission to engage Emily in a conversation. Some diverted to talking to me after their exuberant "Hi!" was met with Emily's unconscious silence. However, others continued to attempt engaging Emily, despite her lack of response. I kept redirecting everyone to speak to me, feeling myself becoming more irritated and worn-out.

I was annoyed by the time 12:15 p.m. rolled around and we finally had our clinic appointment. Emily was wheeled into the small clinic room and again slumped on the couch and closed her eyes, falling asleep. The doctor and nurse tried hard to involve Emily in bubbly conversation. I again explained that not only was she recovering from the general anaesthetic, but she had told us that she was scared of health professionals, and she was naturally a shy child. I suggested it was best to not push a connection with her, and she had asked me directly to ask the doctors and nurses not to talk to her. To all of this, I got the response that I had gotten many times before: "maybe in time she'll warm up to us", because "building rapport is important" and so they would "keep trying". I said nothing, too tired to respond.

The scapegoats

November 2021

It's hard to be angry at God. It's easier to be angry at health professionals. Not openly, of course. But sometimes underneath my polite conversations with them, I respond to them sarcastically in my mind. I feel hyper-vigilant and prickly around them. It is irrational to blame these helpers, these messengers, and yet… sometimes I hate these people who keep touching my daughter or asking me to help them with their invasive treatments. Sometimes I want to scream "no!" in their sweet faces, grab Emily, run out of the hospital and get as far away as possible. But… we're all just stuck here.

Prognosis

December 2021

In the few days after Emily's diagnosis, we had multiple 'bad news' meetings. The amount of new verbal information, presented in medical jargon, was overwhelming.

Short conversations with realistic health professionals are a relief. Emily's surgeon caught us in the hallway one day, and said, "In my experience I've seen kids who've lived six weeks or eighteen months, and anywhere in between. Once you've finished these six weeks of radiotherapy, you'll just be living from scan to scan to find out what will happen for Emily. That's all we can say for sure".

That was it, and B.J. and I both appreciated it, even though it was sobering news. By giving us a realistic window of time, that doctor freed us from having too high hopes or too narrow expectations. It was humble and human advice. Our tired, grieving, and stressed minds could hear it.

It is the "eternal optimist" health professionals who are not preparing us well for the road ahead. Another doctor told B.J. and I that we "had to hope that Emily would be with us for another three or four more years", that she "would be in the 1 per cent", even though the majority of children with Emily's diagnosis die within the first year. We looked at her incredulously; we didn't know if she was lying to us or to herself.

Listening to our family

December 2021

By week four of radiotherapy, Emily is still weeping the entire forty minutes of the journey into the hospital. We were told by a doctor that kids usually start "skipping" into the centre by week four. For Emily, there is no skipping. There are only new tumour symptoms, which we are told is "unusual".

This morning in the waiting room, a doctor was the first health professional to greet me and start the daily hurdle of questions about how Em is going. Em was tucked into my side and hiding her face from him. When I answered honestly about her suffering and her not wanting health professionals to talk to her, he responded gently, "well that's fine, and that's fair enough". He then only spoke to me and kept his questions brief. He impressed me immediately because he was a relief to talk to. He respected what I'd said and did his job quickly and quietly so that Emily felt safe.

We have had a few recovery nurses who approach us in this sensitive way too. These nurses come into the room slowly and softly, sensing or asking about what the best approach is for Emily. They say something to us like, "If you're ok, we won't talk to Emily when she wakes up from the general anaesthetic. She doesn't need a stranger talking to her. We'll sit you next to her, and you can talk to her as she wakes up."

B.J. and I agree readily. These nurses then move quietly and efficiently in the background doing their nursing role and leave us to do our parenting role in peace. I have loved these moments – I love not having a nurse talking over the top of me to Emily as I'm trying to soothe her. These gentle interactions leave me feeling relieved, and Emily is left feeling safe.

The ideal paediatric patient

December 2021

I see some health professionals' expectations for paediatric patients every time I enter the hospital: that children should be playful and extroverted with strangers. They want Em to be chatty, brave, and happy. One of the doctor's shoved his phone in Em's face to show her something he thought was amusing, hoping he'd get a smile from her. Some of the nurses only talk to her in that high pitched, cutesy voice. Some keep trying to chat to her about her sisters or popular kids' fads, even when she is hiding away from them. Some health professionals want her to be the ideal 'cute and compliant' paediatric patient, but instead Em is sad and shy.

I left the house with Emily just after 6:30 a.m. Em sobbed all the way into hospital, telling me many times, "Mummy, I'm scared". I played gentle Psalms music and reached back to hold her hand, which helped a bit, but she still cried quietly to herself. I carried Em into the hospital at 7:30 a.m. In the waiting room, I cuddled Emily and asked her again if she understood why we were doing radiotherapy, and she said she didn't know why. So, I drew her two simple pictures explaining how the radiotherapy light makes the bad sickness in her head get smaller.

This is not the first time I've explained to her the situation, in pictures and words, but Em can't remember. We think the tumour is affecting her short-term memory, and so she looked at the pictures blankly. Emily still doesn't understand the point of radiotherapy, and its week five. And so, snuggled into my arms, turned away from all the health professionals and looking directly into my eyes, she went sadly into another general anaesthetic and radiotherapy.

'Jingle Bells'

December 2021

It's Christmas time in the radiotherapy centre. One of the recovery nurses is wearing fairy lights around her neck and a string of loudly jingling bells around her hands and feet, so she is noisily clanging her way around the radiotherapy department. B.J. and I sit at Emily's bedside, as she is unconscious after radiotherapy, and we are waiting for her to wake up. We murmur to each other quietly about 'Jingle Bells' as we've nicknamed her, feeling dubious about how Emily will take her.

Emily wakes up with moaning and hides under her blankets. We suspect she has another one of her regular headaches, and we try to calm her enough to get her to take some pain relief medicine. 'Jingle Bells' jangles away around Emily's hospital bed, and so Em continues to hide. B.J. and I suggest to 'Jingle Bells' that we have the situation under control, and so she can leave us be. Left alone, in the silence, Em slowly comes out.

The Tide

April 2022

Em was initially looked after by the oncology team. They are a team of optimists and sometimes their constant fighting of cancer makes sense. But I also feel that sometimes they can downplay terminal diagnoses, and the huge cost of fighting.

Two weeks ago, just five months after diagnosis, Emily deteriorated suddenly. Her swallowing became difficult, her speech slurred, and she started crawling around the house instead of walking. From all our reading and prior conversations with Emily's oncology team, B.J. and I were bracing during our next phone call for hearing the words "cancer progression". Instead, the doctor held out hope and encouraged us to fight the cancer harder. We should keep beating against the tide.

The doctor presented us with a huge range of experimental treatments, some based near us, some around the country and still others around the world. There was no one clear treatment to go for; it was up to us to decide. Whether any of them would buy Emily more time, and what the side effects would be, were a grey area. We had to go do our research and then choose.

The doctor didn't realise that I was on the other end of the phone silently sobbing. I was thinking, "How do we decide what to do? What kind of life will that be for Emily? What price do we pay for the slim chance of getting more of her life? How much fighting terminal cancer is 'enough'?"

Emily ultimately answered these questions for us by almost dying about a week later, before suddenly rallying to everyone's surprise. We are now told Em has "days or weeks" to go. Many times, the doctors have told us predictions. In the last two weeks alone, we have been told "she could have maybe eighteen months more to live" or "she could die tonight", but Em is on her own schedule. We don't know how long she has left.

All we know is that all the fighting of Em's cancer is now finally done – we can stop struggling against the tide. And I understand now how utterly blind we all are in evading and predicting death.

7

WALKING BESIDE EMILY

Reflections on my observations of Emily herself, from the time of her diagnosis until her death. Emily was four years old at diagnosis and turned five years old during her cancer treatment.

She did not sing as we did –
It was a different tune –
Herself to her a Music
As Bumble-bee of June.
(Dickinson, 1830–86)

New suffering

October 2021

> "I don't want to be here; I just want to go home. I miss my home."
>
> "Daddy, I would only like it if you were my doctor, then I would be ok."
>
> "I don't like that there's something wrong with me. It's hard."

* * * * *

First week of radiotherapy. It was early Friday morning, moments before we needed to get up for our last trip to the hospital for the week. Emily was lying in bed curled up in a ball of blankets in her "nest" in the living room, awake but more quiet than usual. B.J. came over to her to give her the morning medicines. Emily initially protested, but after gentle but persistent coaxing, she eventually complied.

Em's compliance then gave way to a deep sob. B.J. moved away and I lay down in front of her and held her, with her head nuzzled into my chest. I stroked her hair, and softly intoned for a while. I spoke to her gently. We stayed like that for some minutes more, just holding onto each other in silence. She had a few deep sighs. Then she got up, and her mood shifted. She was a little happier. She was then ready to get her shoes on to go to the hospital for the daily radiotherapy.

Understanding suffering

November 2021

Week three of radiotherapy. In the evening, the older girls were all unsettled and needed extra attention to get to bed. Emily decided she wanted to sleep in the living room "nest" next to me, but then she had to wait for me to settle her sisters. An hour later, I was finally able to join her. Emily had been lying on her side, facing the living room wall. As I lay down next to her, she rolled over and reached out to me, slowly unfolding the load on her mind, "Mummy, I hate radiotherapy".

"I know Darling, it is really hard".

Emily had two large tears in her eyes, but her voice remained steady, "Radiotherapy is really annoying. I don't like going to sleep. The light makes me really tired. I really don't like going".

I held her little body and stroked the hair near her face, "I know Em, it is really hard, I know".

"I don't even know why I'm going".

"Do you remember that there's a sickness in your head, and the light is fighting the sickness? That's why we have to go."

Emily became quiet, and her face was blank. She did not remember. Regardless, she seemed to be finished getting what she needed to off her chest. She asked me to keep holding her. She snuggled in close to my chest and then fell asleep.

* * * * *

December 2021

Em to her sister, chatting over Play-Doh: "Have you ever had radiotherapy?"

Facing Eternity

November 2021

At home, one week after the diagnosis, Emily and I sat at the kitchen bench together, talking about many things. Em was constipated due to her new medications, so I asked her if she would try using the toilet again. Em told me she would try and that she was sure she would be all better again afterwards. I knew what she meant, so I then talked to her about our uncertainty regarding whether she would get better again.

Em started getting teary, "Yeah... You know what's really hard about being a little kid? It's really easy to get hurt when you're a little kid".

Seeing her so vulnerable, I fumbled around to find the right words, "I know hun, it is really hard. I don't know why God is doing this, but it is really hard on you. It's not nice to be in pain. But we know that even though this is happening, we are trusting that God is good".

Em: "Yeah. And you know the good thing about dying is that you get to go be with God."

Me: "Yeah Em, that's right. God is there in heaven, and we'll be right there in heaven with you very soon afterwards."

Em: "But you know the bad thing about dying is that I think it will hurt."

Me: "Yeah… it won't be easy hun… But you know Dad and I, and your sisters, we will never leave you alone. We'll be right there with you. You will never be alone."

Em: "Yeah."

* * * * *

February 2021

During the car trip to school this morning the girls were talking about what you can take with you when you're moving house, and Em said, "I hope I can take Ellie to heaven with me, otherwise I'll miss Ellie."

The older girls were unfazed by her comment, simply saying that you can't take anything to heaven with you, not even favourite toy elephants like Ellie. I had a lump in my throat, seeing my baby contemplate her mortality, and countered, "Well maybe we can ask God to make a special exception for Ellie".

Living in the present

December 2021

Emily loves sorting through her craft supplies and giving her toys new homes in old cardboard boxes. Today she was making a new cardboard bed for "Cushion", one of her mini elephants, and at the same time she talked to me about her plans. She wants to fly a good kite, she wants to ride in a fancy limousine with her cousins, and she even talked about seeing her friends. It was the first time she seemed to have enough energy to think of the future.

Em said, "After I finish radiotherapy next week, then I will be all better again".

I replied cautiously, "Em, we can pray that that will happen, but we don't know if you'll ever get fully better again. But you might feel better for a while, or you might be healed, or you might get sick again later on. We just have to take each day as it comes. Whatever happens, God is with us."

Em remained hopeful, "I think I'm going to get better".

* * * * *

February 2022

Em started school last week with the adults around her deciding when she was too tired and needed to go home. She stayed at school for an hour. Yet it was hard to know what she wanted to do. So, with her teacher's blessing, I made Em a desktop chart so that she can point to different pictures to tell the teacher how she feels and when she would like to go home.

Her teacher trialled it today and Em stayed in class for two hours instead of the usual one. As I carried her in my arms out of the school, I asked her if she was tired. Em smiled, "Yeah, but I kept pointing to the green picture because I want to stay at school, even though I'm actually tired". "So, you had a good day?" I asked. Em replied, "Yeah, I played with my friends".

* * * * *

March 2022

Em's Starlight Foundation 'Make A Wish' was for a 'milkshakes by the pool' holiday for five days. We made it to the holiday, but Em is deteriorating quickly now, and B.J. and I are carrying her everywhere as she struggles to get a full breath. We went to the pool on the first day and realised that Em can no longer swim. So, she sat in the shallows watching her sisters swim, and the older girls played a pretend fishing game with her.

We went to a tourist shop on the second day, and Em was immediately drawn to a large squirt gun. So now we sit her in the shallows of the pool, and Em spends a large part of her time squirting water at her sisters. She asks them to bob up and down, and then she hunts them down, smacking them with the water right in their faces. She lets out her deep, husky giggle each time she gets them.

Control

March 2022

Today Em went to the hospital for the oncology clinic before her MRI tomorrow. The MRI is our first check since radiotherapy ended just over two months ago to see whether there is any growth in the tumour. Em hates hospital appointments, often saying she is scared and that she feels that "other people" are making her go. When she came home from the hospital this afternoon, her new living room day bed had just arrived, so I helped her set it up. Em was very excited; it is her new "nest".

When her sisters got home from school this afternoon to try out the nest, Em immediately asserted her authority over it. She started letting them know that there were "nest rules": no craft in her nest, no kicking her out of her nest, and no jumping on her nest.

B.J. and I went out to the backyard to talk about the plan for the week, and then when we came back inside the girls were playing a dressing up game of 'Queen'. The girls were draped in an array of scarves, skirts, and dresses. Emily was the 'Queen' on her day bed nest throne, and she had her older sisters setting up a banquet of pretend food in front of her. The older girls spent the afternoon serving the 'Queen' in her new nest.

Grieving life

April 2022

Em was sitting up in the bed in her room this afternoon, and I laid out food options for her to have a snack. We're one month into this 'final stage' and her swallow has deteriorated so much that I could only lay out thickened, puree and dissolvable food options for her. Em screwed up her face and asked me for different food, and I had to tell her that this was the only food that was safe for her now. This made her upset. She asked me to leave her, and I said

I couldn't go because I had to watch her eat to make sure she was safe. This made her even angrier. She shuffled away from me then. In her slow, slurred speech she laid out her reasons for sorrow:

"I'm cranky now. I can't eat anything, I can't go to Grandma's for a sleepover, I can't go in the car, I can't go to the shops, I can't walk, I just have to stay here forever, sick till I die. And I won't have Ellie in heaven, I won't have anyone to huggle me." She stared intensely at me, crying angrily.

I had started crying, so then we stared at each other, both crying. I responded sorrowfully, "I know Darling, I know, I'm sad too. I can't fix any of this and it makes me so sad. The only thing I can say is that God says that in heaven you will be happy. And I will be coming there right behind you. But I am so sad too, and I will miss you."

Em then broke down sobbing and moved towards me to climb into my arms. I lifted her into my lap, and we wept together. We hugged each other and nuzzled our faces together. After some time, she sighed. She had let it out. She was then happy for the rest of the evening.

Softened

April 2022

Before the cancer, Em was a huge ball of energy and fun, though stubborn. Now she is in this 'final stage' a fatigue has settled over her, and we often suspect she is having headaches that she can't express to us. Her eyes don't seem to be focusing. The steroids medication also makes Em irritable. She struggles to walk. Aside from all the physical symptoms, she is also scared and sad. All of this means that at times Em can be short-tempered, demanding, and insatiably hungry.

But lately she seems to be becoming more aware of her impact on us. She now initiates reaching out to us, saying, "I'm sorry I get cranky with you Daddy" or "I'm sorry I always ask you for food Mummy". We readily reassure her and comfort her, talking her through it. But I see her spirit is softening and opening to us, even as her suffering is increasing.

* * * * *

April 2022
Em was incontinent overnight and woke up this morning more slurred in her words, looking more weak and tired. Each new, small loss of this achingly slow 'final stage' of the cancer is heart-breaking. So, when B.J. carried her into our bed for a rest at about 5 a.m., I had a quiet cry beside her. She saw me crying, and so put her hand on me to comfort me and said, "Mummy, I'm not that worried about dying. I'm just super cranky that Ellie isn't coming with me to heaven."

Getting ready

May 2022
After six weeks of slow decline, Em seemed to be sensing her end is finally coming. She asked me if I could throw her a party with the family in the week before my birthday. She asked to pick the decorations and cake, and she helped me make a 'pass the parcel'. She asked me to help her make a collection of 'Ellie' elephant bookmarks to be given out within the family. So, we had the last family birthday celebrations together and we made her last 'Ellie' craft together.

Finally, one of her last conversations was with her Daddy. She has sometimes pushed B.J. away recently, and their relationship has been strained at times as she has often clung to me. Yet, her final setting into order of her life, her telling of her hope of heaven, and her tender instructions for us to all look after each other after she leaves us, were all given privately to B.J.. One last special father and daughter moment. Soon afterwards, she fell asleep, and has now woken up again into this 'locked in' syndrome, unable to speak.

"Sad, Hug"

May 2022

My beautiful girl, snuggled into my chest. Limp, and everyday draining of more life. B.J. and I rotate with her around the living room to different positions, holding her or staying near to her. B.J. pours over what medications to give her and when. We have just switched over to tube feeding her, as she can no longer swallow. Em has 'locked in' syndrome, so she is unable to move, and is cycling through naps and watching TV. We ask her what she needs through us pointing at a booklet of pictures we have made up for her. For the last few days, the only pictures she blinks 'yes' to is, "sad, hug". She is leaving us.

8

BEING GRATEFUL

Reflections regarding the gifts suffering can bring, from a few months after Emily's death.

When my mother died, I inherited her needlepoint tapestries. When I was a little boy, I used to sit at her feet as she worked on them. Have you ever seen needlepoint from underneath?
All I could see was chaos; strands of thread all over with no seeming purpose. As I grew, I was able to see her work from above. I came to appreciate the patterns, the need for the dark threads as well as the light and gaily colored ones.
Life is like that. From our human perspective, we cannot see the whole picture, but we should not despair or feel that there is no purpose. There is meaning and purpose even for the dark threads, but we cannot see that right away.
(Cohen, p. 31)

Trees

May 2022

We sat around for family devotions last night in our family of four now, only one week since Em has passed away. Reflecting on Isaiah 61:3 and how God grows us as trees, I asked the two older girls to summarise the last two and a half years. For both girls, these years have been the early primary school years.

L. immediately answered, "Well remember first there was that drought, and we couldn't use much water. Then there was fires everywhere, with smoke blocking the sun. Then there was COVID for two years, and lockdown and home school. Then Emily got sick and died. So basically, in life, something bad will happen, until the next bad thing happens."

Her summary stunned us all initially. I immediately saw how my children's childhood is turning out to be harder than my own was. All the "bad things" she had listed – natural disasters, a global pandemic, sickness, and death – I had not been able to shield her or her sisters from any of these things. All we could do was turn as a family again to our faith and hang onto the promises of God to sustain us:

"God has promised to plant us as trees, giving us roots deep enough to hold on through the storm. Daddy and I will always try to be there for you both, but ultimately, only

God is the One who is going to be with you both through your whole lives and into eternity. We trust that God holds us four on earth, and He holds Emily in heaven, safe."

The well-worn road

June 2022

> …Behold, we know not anything;
> I can but trust that good will fall
> At last – far off – at last, to all,
> And every winter change to spring.
> So runs my dream: but what am I?
> An infant crying in the night:
> An infant crying for the light:
> And with no language but a cry.
> (Tennyson, p. LIV)

Three weeks since Em has left us, and her loss is so heavy and bewildering. A few times now I have been teary about Em around a friend, and they have said in response, "Em's in heaven now and you'll be with her again". Those words are not always as comforting as they think it is, or as I thought it would be. They feel like a steadying anchor for my soul, but also a far-off happiness – it may be fifty years until I see her again.

Right now, I am more comforted by reminders that suffering is a well-worn road. Reaching out to a God who has suffered is comforting. Reaching out to a community, past and present, to hear other stories of suffering is also a comfort. In listening to others, I can see my situation from many angles, with many different words, and I can feel a family around me. Others may not have the same story, but all have their own deep aches eventually.

While I was out with my mum this week, I ran into an old friend, and she shared with me sadly of her struggles to have children. I shared my loss of a child, and my mum quietly cried beside us as I spoke of Emily, weeping for her granddaughter. All three of us trusted God with our sorrow, and yet the sorrows were unresolved and tender. This gentle moment of different yet shared loss and faith was deeply soothing to me.

Presence

July 2022

This experience of inescapable and unrelenting suffering stopped all action.

There was no place to go, nowhere to hide, no route left to take. Nothing to do but surrender to sickness and death as it overcame our little one. Initially, we tried to fight for her, but eventually we had to let go. All we could do was be present for her and be humbled by our own powerlessness. To sit still. Witness. Cradle her as she slowly left.

Sometimes there is nothing more to do or to say, only to be present.

Treasure

July 2022

Yesterday we came home to see that a storm had blown off one of our small pots from the back patio table. Dirt and pottery were strewn all over the ground. As I looked closer, it was the Mother's Day gift pot that Em had painted for me last year, with a small succulent plant she'd planted inside. On the bottom of a pottery shard, I could see 'Emily' marked on top of the silver and bronze paint she'd chosen.

Initially I shrugged it off as I put away some other things first. But once I got to cleaning it up, the finality of the shattered pottery pieces hit me. "Em can't just make me a new 'Mother's Day' pot; this gift from her is just broken now". I sobbed more and more deeply as I re-potted the small succulent plant into another of my favourite pots. By the time I was trying to super glue Emily's pot back together, my hands were shaking. I couldn't see through the tears, and I was super gluing my fingers to the glue tube.

I had to stop and calm down. The pot and the plant were as 'fixed' as I could make them, but essentially, they were broken. Life is broken now. Em's time on this earth is over, and her earthly things were not made to last. It is hard to hold them with an open hand, not enshrining them, knowing they may irretrievably break down. It is going to be like this throughout the years now, until I get to heaven. I will have to continually let Emily go on this earth.

I am now seeing Matthew 6:20-21 in a new light, which says, "But store up for yourselves treasures in heaven... For where your treasure is, there your heart will be also." The deep ache I feel for Em is softened when I see her as one of my treasures in heaven. I am on my way there, so although I still mourn her here, I can also look beyond what is broken in the present.

A different view

July 2022

My faith has changed because of Emily's suffering. Our faith is built around a story of great suffering. And now I know something more of what it is like to have anguished prayers for relief answered with 'no'. I have seen some of the crushing intensity of suffering. I understand more about sorrows that are beyond tears and words. I know what it is like to be a watching, horrified parent. I see more of the brokenness of the world; I have felt first-hand the deep fracture in creation. So, I feel my faith has a closer view on this story now.

But simultaneously, my faith feels more human and fragile. I feel more hesitant in prayer now, because of the giant 'no' we received. And life itself feels more precarious and mysterious than ever before.

Understanding heaven

July 2022

The older girls are full of questions about where their sister is, and what exactly she is doing. With a deep, vested interest now, we are having to explain what we trust in faith about Emily in eternity. Some of the questions and comments from the older girls are:

"Mum, I wonder if Em is setting up her room now in heaven?"

"I wonder if God gave her a brand-new Ellie?"

"I wonder what crafts Emily is doing right now?"

"Do you think Emily still sleeps in heaven?"

"Do you think Emily needs to eat anything in heaven?"

"When we get to heaven, Emily can show us around everywhere".

> She is not sent away, but only sent before, like unto a star, which going out of our sight doth not die and evanish, but shineth in another hemisphere. Ye see her not, yet she doth shine in another country. (Rutherford, p. 41)

Poured out

August 2022

This experience has given me a different understanding of certain expressions, such as what it means for a person to be 'poured out' in service (Phil. 2:17). I have never felt more poured out than when we gave almost everything in those final weeks; B.J. and I were almost completely emptied of ourselves in order to carry Emily through her death. Our two older daughters poured themselves out daily for months to serve their younger sister. Emily's health professionals continually poured themselves out, day in and day out at the hospital, in often thankless jobs. Our community and our families poured themselves out to love and surround us during Emily's cancer and death. 'Poured out' is a lived experience for us now.

Death again

August 2022

Its three months today since Em has passed, and another death is now upon us. For the last few days, my mum and I have been visiting daily and sitting at the nursing home bedside of my mum's mum – Nan. The generations are pulled together at a death bed again.

The rhythms of death are now more familiar to us, having seen it up close with Emily in our home. We follow through similar routines again now: trying to make her comfortable, wondering about the long gaps between breaths, long conversations with the nurses, stroking her hand and her hair, and lots of sitting together. We know more about what to ask the nurses, we understand more about what we are seeing, and we feel calmer in being close to Nan and caring for her. We are better companions for Nan.

Mum and I are also better companions for each other. We are sandwiched in-between the generations, with loss at either end. We can now carry a lot more of the load for each other.

Gifts

June 2022

B.J. and I lay around and listened to the rain on Sunday afternoon. B.J.'s tears fell freely; he feels Emily everywhere in our house and he misses her. He talked about the way suffering can discipline the soul. He feels that he now holds onto his faith more dearly than ever before. He also feels he is a different doctor now: more aware of patients' suffering and more attune to their grief. Both deep changes could not have happened without Em.

I agree, and I have also changed. I feel that I struggled for a long time with feeling like an angry failure for not being able to save Em. I think I was, deep down, holding onto the Western expectation of progression and optimism in life. I had unconsciously hoped that if I had enough knowledge and connections as a health professional, my children would be safe. That my Emily would, in general, have a good life if I worked hard enough for her. I feel I hadn't allowed for this life to be as truly broken and uncontrollable as it is. So, I feel humbled. And I now feel more open to the whole story: to life *and* death, and the ultimate hope our faith offers.

We both feel deep changes already beginning in us, and Em has only been gone for a month. Her worthy legacy now stretches out beyond us in this life. Yet, we also feel deeply

– and permanently – sad. We will always miss her. There is so much unanswered and unresolved, and honestly, we would both much rather have Emily herself here. Still, we will treasure the gifts that God gives to us because of her.

Acknowledgements

Given that I have tried to protect many people's privacy within this book, it is difficult now to openly acknowledge many of those same people. I believe that I have tried to thank most of you in person, so I trust that you know who you are in these sometimes-cloaked comments.

We are truly appreciative to all the health professionals who have worked with our family, particularly when we were so constantly stressed and in grief. Thank you to all our friends for their generosity and thoughtfulness to us. To our church families, your ongoing prayers, support, and the tears you shared with us are greatly cherished. To Emily's teachers and everyone at our children's school, our deepest thanks. You made Emily's time at school so special, and you never tired of finding ways to support our family. Thank you especially to Emily's school friends, who brightened her hardest days. Thank you to all who still remember Emily with us.

We acknowledge the incredible support we have from our parents and extended families, who have all gone above and beyond to take care of us. A special thanks to Emily's cousins, who were her dearest friends. Thank you to my husband, B.J., for walking this terrible road with me and for always finding a way to keep going. Thank you to my two eldest daughters, for your patience and for allowing me to share my perspective on our stories.

I am grateful to the close friends and family who gave their feedback on the initial versions of this book. Thank you especially to my Mum and Dad, for your advice and encouragement in this process. Thank you to Christian Focus, for your support and for publishing this book. A heartfelt thanks to Megan Best for generously writing the foreword and for your continued support.

Finally, special thanks are sent heavenward. Firstly, to my youngest daughter, Emily, for all you are to me and for all you have taught me. Lastly, thank you to God – for the hope You have given us to endure this.

References

Alcott, L. M. (1868-9). *Little Women* (2018 ed.). New York: Penguin Books.

Bayly, J. (1969). *The Last Thing We Talk About* (1985 ed.). Elgin, IL: David C. Cook Publishing Co.

Cohen, K. L. (2011). In J. Lynn, Harrold, J., & Schuster, J.L. (Ed.), *Handbook for mortals: Guidance for People Facing Serious Illness* (2 ed.). Oxford: Oxford University Press.

Dickinson, E. (1830-1886). One sister have I in our house. *Academy of American Poets, accessed 22 August 2022, https://poets.org/poem/one-sister-have-i-our-house-14.*

Eliot, G. (1860). *The Mill on the Floss* (1999 ed.). Hertfordshire, U.K.: Wordsworth Classics.

Frankl, V. E. (1946). *Man's Search for Meaning* (2008 ed.). London: Rider.

Getty, K., Townend, S., Kauflin, J., & Sherman Merker, M. (2018). I will wait for you (Psalm 130). Nashville: Getty Music Publishing (BMI).

Lewis, C. S. (1961). *A Grief Observed* (2013 ed.). London: Faber and Faber Limited.

McKelvey, D. (2021). *Every Moment Holy* (Vol. 2). Nashville: Rabbit Room Press.

Paterson, K. (1977). *Bridge to Terabithia* (2015 ed.). UK: Puffin Books.

Poe, E. A. (1849). A dream within a dream. In *The Complete Illustrated Works of Edgar Allan Poe* (2013 ed.). London: Bounty Books.

Rutherford, S. (1664). *Letters of Samuel Rutherford* (1996 ed.). Edinburgh: The Banner of Truth Trust.

Taylor, A. (1782–1866). My sister. In R. Cope, Harris, A. & Hinckley, J. (Ed.), *Family Life in England and America, 1690-1820* (2021 ed.). ebook: Routledge.

Tennyson, A. (1849). *In Memoriam A.H.H.* (2018 ed.). Sydney, Australia: Amazon.

Tolstoy, L. (1886). *The Death of Ivan Ilych* (L. Maude, Trans. 2019 ed.). Bulgaria: Demetra Publishing.

Wolterstorff, N. (1987). *Lament for a Son*. Michigan: Wm. B. Eerdmans Publishing Co.

Wordsworth, W. (1798). The education of nature. In F. T. Palgrave (Ed.), *The Golden Treasury of English Verse (1861)* (2011 ed.). London: Macmillian Collector's Library.

Also available from Christian Focus ...

HEAVEN, HOW I GOT HERE

THE STORY OF THE THIEF ON THE CROSS

COLIN S. SMITH

Heaven, How I Got Here

The Story of the Thief on the Cross

Colin S. Smith

What if you woke up one morning knowing that it was your last day on earth? That's what happened to the thief on the cross, who died a few feet from Jesus. *Heaven, How I Got Here* is his story, told in his own words, as he looks back from Heaven on the day that changed his eternity, and the faith that can change yours.

Here is a gripping account of God's amazing grace that comes alive as recounted from this unusual and really helpful perspective.

Alistair Begg
Senior Pastor, Parkside Church
Chagrin Falls, Ohio

Christian Focus Publications

Our mission statement

Staying Faithful

In dependence upon God we seek to impact the world through literature faithful to His infallible Word, the Bible. Our aim is to ensure that the Lord Jesus Christ is presented as the only hope to obtain forgiveness of sin, live a useful life and look forward to heaven with Him.

Our Books are published in four imprints:

CHRISTIAN FOCUS

Popular works including biographies, commentaries, basic doctrine and Christian living.

MENTOR

Books written at a level suitable for Bible College and seminary students, pastors, and other serious readers. The imprint includes commentaries, doctrinal studies, examination of current issues and church history.

CHRISTIAN HERITAGE

Books representing some of the best material from the rich heritage of the church.

CF4KIDS

Children's books for quality Bible teaching and for all age groups: Sunday school curriculum, puzzle and activity books; personal and family devotional titles, biographies and inspirational stories – because you are never too young to know Jesus!

Christian Focus Publications Ltd,
Geanies House, Fearn, Ross-shire,
IV20 1TW, Scotland, United Kingdom.
www.christianfocus.com